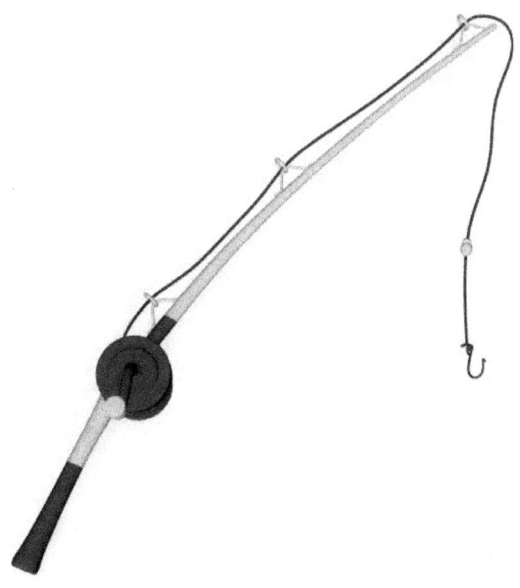

Land It!

*Job Hunting Tips
for Prime of Lifers*

Patty DeDominic

www.thenewnewworldofwork.com

DeDominic & Associates

Helping Achievers Soar

Published by
DeDominic & Associates
2353 E. Valley Rd.
Santa Barbara, CA 93108
805-565-9967
DeDominic.com

Dedication

I wrote this book to help you clarify the key steps in getting better job offers. You have already proven you can be a good student. Now that you are ready to join tax payer status, congratulations!

My advice is not for everybody. Some may try to complicate the job hunt or claim special knowledge is needed for certain professions. While this book cannot cover all of the minute details and job scenarios you may face, it does deliver principles for your success. If you follow these tips and guidelines you will put yourself out in front of 90% of the other job hunters and you will get better job offers.

I owe special thanks to my research and publishing assistant, Miss Inderjit Kaur; awesome Art Director, TooFun Sue; and to Angela Barbero and Matt Laband of DeDominic & Associates for editorial help.

Patty DeDominic

Foreword

I've got some tips for you to put to work today. This book shows you how to increase your hire-ability immediately. Wouldn't it be nice if you could learn how to evaluate yourself more objectively and effectively? Want to learn better ways to ask for feedback and help? You can set yourself on a path to your next career move with more confidence.

Are you ready? Ready to reinvent your future? This book CAN help you build your self-confidence, and prepare you for the realities for the job hunt in 2012 and beyond.

Set some goals and employ time tested success techniques. Once you can imagine your goals, you are closer to creating your ideal future. You'll be able to create action steps for reaching new opportunities and better job offers.

Patty DeDominic
Coach to High Achievers
Dedominic.com

'I'm in the prime of life, and never thought I would have to look for a new job now.'

Does this sound like you or someone you know?
Are you ready to leverage your life experience?
Would you like to reignite your power?
Find that spark that got you your first job?

If you answered 'YES', this book is for you.

Prime of Lifers ask:

'How long will it take me to find a job?'

'How can I put myself out in front of the competition?'

'How do I get called back for interviews?'

I will answer these questions here. I started and built a successful Los Angeles based recruiting firm. For over twenty years we heard and answered these questions, for over one million job applicants. I'm the founder of PDQ Careers and helped grow CT Engineering, which we purchased and later sold. During my years as a CEO we placed over 250,000 people and learned what it takes to get hired. Let me give you some new tools and techniques now.

You will be able to tap into time tested Tips for Success. We developed these tip and strategies while working with prestigious clients such as: Wells Fargo Bank, AutoDesk, the Microsoft Corporation, the Auto Clubs, the American Red Cross, AT&T, USC, Universal and Paramount Studios, children's hospitals and governments.

The 7 Things
You Need to Know!

Your Network = Your Net-worth

References – Life Long

Looking for a Job is a Full Time Job

Social Media Counts

New Jobs are Invented Daily

Job Clubs – Yes!

Price Matters – Volunteer &
Internships Pay Off

Key Skills & Values for 2020

Resiliency

Creativity

Resourcefulness

Integrity

Perpetual Learner

Vision Holder

Illuminator

Ability to Live With Rapid Change
and Ambiguity

GETTING GOOD JOB OFFERS

Getting good job offers is like accomplishing most other goals, except it's harder.

Because job hunting is so personal, it's harder to be objective. Being objective as well as professional in your job search is important. I want to help you unlock your personal power. Yes, your power is in there...waiting for you to shine your light and show off *your* talents.

Are you ready?

I remember my first job hunt; it was frustrating and confusing, though eventually it was successful.

Maybe you are like me? When I was a teenager I was just hoping someone, anyone, would hire me. I just couldn't wait to get out there and talk to people, to find the lucky person who would become my employer. For weeks it seemed there were no takers!

When I started in the job hunt game for the first time as a 16 year old, it seemed so unfair that all the employers wanted experience. How was I supposed to get experience if employers were only hiring people with experience? It was a Catch-22.

My friends got hired, why didn't I get those offers too? I had some lessons to learn and plenty of doors to knock on. I didn't give up even though each 'no offer' or 'no openings' seemed like a personal rejection. Ouch!

Luckily someone did hire me, eventually. Mrs. DeWeese and Mrs. Opotowski were willing to give me the chance I needed. I learned a lot from these wonderful women, even if I was just their babysitter. First jobs, no matter what they are can make a lifetime impact and can teach valuable life lessons. These two women were model moms and homemakers. I got to help them and they helped me refine my ideals and learn working skills.

Fast-forward 30+ years. Plenty has changed, but the enduring principles of success have not.

Let's start now to help you get that wonder and excitement back, it's important! With focus and effort you can put life back into your job search. You'll soon employ new brain and attitude "muscles" and learn new skills. You'll need them.

Is this simple? Not exactly, but remember, you did get your first job. If a new graduate or a teenager can do this, so can you!

Will it be stressful? Probably! Learning anything new will create some anxiety, but you can soon replace fear and anxiety with new knowledge and confidence. You can practice your success recipes on your personal network first. Then when refined, you can take them on the road. If you put your game face on and believe that this is a magical journey for self-empowerment, it will be!

Recipe for Job Success*

3 parts Willingness to Learn & Grow
3 parts Hard Work
2 parts Contemporary Skills & Experience
2 parts Ability to Communicate & Focus
2 parts Strong Network
1 part Personal Inventory/Self Awareness
1 part Luck

Mix ingredients and let sit, but not for too long. Proceed with your job hunt. Tweak recipe as needed for your industry, salary range, and geography.

Add mentors & go!
Apply yourself furiously.
Focus on your dream job and your professional goals.

VOILA! Job Success! You've Landed It!

*Implementation & execution time may vary.
<u>Do</u> try this at home.

About this 'Success Recipe'

You can put this recipe to work immediately. When you use it strategically it will enhance your earning power and your life.

So, go ahead, get ready to take a closer look at yourself. But do not get too comfy. This book is meant to be read while standing, or better yet, while on the run! You will need to get polished up a bit...rev up your enthusiasm, bolster your confidence and shine your own light! Start out by lining up some help for yourself. You are not in this alone! It is much more fun to share your successes and learnings with others.

It Takes A Team to Land Great Opportunities

It's going to take a team and you will be building a support network. You can call this your own personal job lead pipeline and you'll soon fill it with people who can help you and whom you can help in return. This is an important part of your success recipes.

Test this and you will soon see if you are half-baked or ready to go! We want to help you become fully baked (meaning competitive and job ready). Not only able to get job offers, but being able to add real value to your own pipeline and that of others. This keeps you not just employed, but more competitive and in demand.

Today's Employers Want to *Have Their Cake* and *Eat it Too!* Don't Offer Yourself Only Half-baked.

'Fully baked? How will I know when I am ready? I was hoping to be already done years ago!'

You will know when you are ready because more people will refer job leads to you. Offers will start coming in as soon as you begin to unlock your personal power. The better prepared you are, the more options you will have. Let us show you how to get lucky at this game called the Job Hunt.

Job Hunting 101 Checklist

I created a short Job Hunting Checklist. This will help you gauge how much homework you will have. Each person has his or her own criteria for a satisfactory job. No matter what your benchmark, you can increase your options and *Land It* faster.

Give yourself one point for each check mark. Most people score 5 or less when they make their first call or email to get an interview. If you score 7 or less, you have your work cut out for you. If you score 8-9 then you can be ready in two days or less. If you score 10*, congratulations! You are well on your way to receiving successful job offers.

*If you score a perfect 10, consider becoming an employment coach; a profession that will always be in demand..

Job Hunting 101 Checklist

Check all that apply:

☐ Objective Clarified

☐ Resume & Cover Letter

☐ Resume & Cover Letter Proofread Twice

☐ References Prepared

☐ Computer Skills Updated

☐ Transportation & Communication Arranged

☐ Prepared and Able to Work

☐ Strengths and Weaknesses Defined

☐ Proper Attire for the Job

☐ Attitude Adjusted and Focused

☐ Mentors or Job Counselors Consulted

☐ Elevator Pitch Ready

Tally Your Score: _____

Checklist Assessment

After your own Job Hunting Checklist assessment, have your mentors, friends, or spouse rate you on the Job Hunting Checklist.

How well do you know yourself?_____
_____

How does your score compare to the score they gave you?_____
_____

Do you have work to do?_____
If so, list what:
- _____
- _____
- _____

Do your mentors know you any better after this exercise?_____

If not, why not?_____
_____
_____

If yes, congratulations! You can help us write the next book! Please send us an email and let us know how you did! coach@dedominic.com

Q:

What are the key steps in the successful job hunt?

A:

Prepare Yourself

1. Plan your approach.

2. Identify your preferred industry, locale and job.

3. Clarify your personal priorities, needs & wants.

4. Present yourself.

5. Follow up!

6. Reel in the offers.

7. Land It! (close the deal)

8. Start the job and deliver value everyday!

9. Learn a lot and have fun.

Q:

Where do I start?

A:

Warm referrals
are the best!

Ask your friends and local business people for referrals. One of our favorite sources for cold job leads today is Craigslist. You can find thousands of jobs on-line.

We are also seeing notices posted in stores windows and on company websites. Job openings are everywhere. Learn to mine them to find your gold and don't forget to share some of the leads with your peer job circle. You never know who is just waiting for that referral from you!

Update your social media profiles, and ask for recommendations. Check to make sure your Facebook and other social media sites are consistent with a professional image of someone hirable.

Investigate Monster.com, Craigslist, or any other job posting website specific to your city.

Q:

How long will this job hunt take?

A:

How fast can you learn and how flexible are you?

There isn't one answer for the prime of life job hunter. Some people get call backs and job offers their first day out. Others may take weeks or even months to customize their approach. One thing is for sure, you will get signs of your job suitability immediately.

Emails not pinging? This will take some time. There used to be a rule of thumb:a professional would most likely be out of work at least one month for every ten thousand dollars they earned. A person earning $70,000 annually might expect to take seven months to complete a successful job search and get back to work. That rule was common before the internet brought the world to our desktops.

We Live in a 24/7/365 Wired World

Today's employers have global options and 24-hour availability of support. The far reaching recessions of the past few years turned the old ways of job hunting upside down! That's why I want to remind you, the economy and jobs scene is reinventing itself right now. There really is a whole new world of work.

Your speed of offers depends on many variables including: your geography, pay, skills, and competition. Your attitude, self-motivation, and actions will speed your job hunt. Want to cut the time in half, or get job offers next week? Then read and apply these success recipes today!

Q:

Aren't some people
just luckier
at this game?

What part does
luck play?

A:

Luck does play a part in job search success.

We want you to be able to increase your luck. Your success depends on how qualified, prepared and focused you are. Some people think that others have better luck in job hunts. We know you make lots of your own luck and the more focused and prepared you are, the luckier you get!

ADVICE IN
A
NUTSHELL

Q:

I'm intimidated by the job-hunting process. Any advice in a nutshell?

A:

Enjoy the journey.

If you prepare yourself and make the decision to be proactive, you will soon receive good job offers. The job hunt is a wonderful opportunity to learn and connect with great new people.

1. Assemble your necessary documents* and support team.

2. Create and review your elevator pitch, your brag sheet. (see next page)

3. Research job leads and do outreach. Connect and follow up.

4. Apply online and in person every day. Job hunting is a numbers game so keep your pipeline full.

5. Every action and interview is a learning opportunity.

6. Follow up and don't give up!

*Documents may include resume, diplomas, non-confidential work samples, certificates, letters of reference, social security and identity or legal right to work.

Q:

What is an Elevator Pitch?

A:

Your 30-60 second upbeat commercial introduction.

An elevator pitch is your short story that can be used whenever you meet new people. Think of what you might say in the time it takes to ride an elevator up to the 10th floor. Practice your pitch in front of the mirror, and for friends until it sounds great. Keep it real.

One might go like this:

'Hi my name is John; I am a former marine with management and technology skills. I am looking for a new job in a law office where I can apply my administrative skills and passion for justice. I've returned to school and hope to get my Law degree in another year.'

Q:

Why would any company want my skills and me?

A:

This is a very important question to ask, and answer before you begin applying for jobs.

Take a personal inventory of your skills, education and qualities. Think about your past experiences and your accomplishments. Translate them into assets.

Launch your courage, and without being too boastful, make a list of ways you can contribute. Know that employers are likely to be interested in confident, hopeful employees, who have a proven track record of contributions. Enterprises need good employees and collaborators who will help them serve their clients. Your part will be to demonstrate how you can do that for your next employer!

Q:

What are today's employers *really* looking for?

A:

There really is no *one right* answer to that question, each employer is unique.

There are, of course, some fundamentals that almost all employers agree on:

- Ready, willing and able to work.
- Clean, well-groomed appearance.
- Good work ethic.
- Optimistic and can do attitude.
- Low maintenance personality.
- Contemporary skills and mind set.
- Work and play well with others.
- Good cultural fit.
- People who add value to the company.

Q:

How can I stand out from the thousands of other job hunters?

A:

Standing out from other applicants can be difficult.

However, you likely have a set of characteristics and skills that make you stand out. It is helpful to recognize the strengths and weaknesses of other professionals in your chosen industry. If you can identify those things, then it becomes much easier to recognize how you are unique.

Interviewing is a good way to stand out from the rest of the applicants. Keep a positive attitude, be energetic and lively, do not speak in a monotone voice, and demonstrate that you are a motivated go-getter. Avoid sob stories; it is a tough job market for everyone. Employers really don't want to hear about the hardships you have been facing in your employment search, or your personal life. This is a professional interview, do not get too personal; even if your interviewer seems friendly and personable.

Keep your problems to yourself.
Everyone has life challenges.
Remember never air
your dirty laundry at work,
or a job interview.

Beware of Pity Parties

"Try to stand out from all others; find what your unique strength is and then use it to be innovative. Employers like innovative employees who think about what extra they can do, not just what they have been told to do."

Jim Delshad
CEO, American International Business Technology, Inc.
Mayor of Beverly Hills (2011)

Q:

How much following up should I do?

A:

Persistence has been shown to have a positive effect in almost *any endeavor.*

Use good judgment for each potential employer, but don't be afraid to *go for it* with persistence if you feel you could contribute to a company and their mission. Most applicants will simply give up when they receive a rejection; however, the truly determined will not stop there.

Perhaps an employer hired someone who is not working out. Your optimistic, enthusiastic follow up, sincere thanks, and expression of continued interest could pay dividends.

"Be persistent, follow your heart. You spend a great deal of time at work, so be sure to choose an industry you enjoy and a company you respect. If you don't succeed in capturing the attention of a company you like, don't give up. Try creative approaches to get their attention. Persistence usually pays off."

Paul Orfalea
**Founder and former Chair of the Board,
KINKO's**

Q:

How important is it to update my computer and Internet research skills?

A:

Computer literacy is essential!

Your computer and Internet skills are as important today as having a telephone was when we were growing up. Don't think you can skip this basic skill, you can't.

Make technology and the Internet your friend. Proclaiming you are a Luddite will not help you! Skills we consider essential today include being able to find your way around internet search engines, and the software for your industry or profession (see appendix for a list of computer essentials).

Almost every job uses technology in some way. Even gardeners, housekeepers and old economy workers need computers. Not long ago, I was at a new hotel, which hired over eleven hundred employees; every one of them applied online. Millions of jobs are out there, in fact it is likely you will find your next job online.

*See appendix for a list of computer essentials

Q:

Can I update *my skills* at home?

A:

YES!

You can search the Internet for journals, online classes and webinars. Do all you can to brush up your skills, and build up your confidence.

Today there are numerous online skills enhancement opportunities. A number of accredited universities now offer degree programs completely online. A recent Google search netted over 200 accredited schools offering both degrees and training online.

Take classes if you don't know how to use a computer. Find good classes at your local community college, online and through your state Employment Development Department's One-Stop office, www.careeronestop.org.

There are other alternatives available, such as Lynda.com, one of the fastest growing educational companies in the United States.

Q:

Can I use
government resources?

A:

Absolutely!
Get some dividends for
your tax payer status.

Visit your local Employment Development Department (EDD) or the One Stop for job listings and coaching. Your local EDD gives access to job listings, feedback on your resume, can review your skill sets, and include you in support groups.

Most government grants will come in the form of unemployment insurance, benefits, or job counseling, and EDD workshops.

The U.S. Department of Labor website can direct you to the One Stop in your state. Billions of tax dollars have been invested in this resource, use it to your advantage. www.dol.gov/dol/jobs.htm.

In California, you can find this resource at: www.caljobs.ca.gov.

Q:

Do job clubs really help?

A:

Yes, if you become part of a network of people who refer job leads to each other.

A strong network can help you fill your prosperity pipeline. Most people have heard of the hidden job market. Interviewers place a lot of weight on referrals from people they trust. Hiring data shows that referrals, not classified ads, are responsible for over 80% of new job starts.

Your network is often directly connected to your net worth. Even if you don't aspire to become rich, learn to build a quality network; enrich it, and your network will better nurture you!

Invest in yourself by making plenty of pay it forward deposits. Think alumni connections, your church, professional associations and conferences. Tend your in-person and online networks, and they will return dividends a plenty.

Q:

With employers asking us to apply online **are resumes still needed?**

A:

Your Resume
is your calling card,
make it a good one!

Keep your resume updated, online, and printed on nice paper. Your resume is often your admission ticket. Like a driver's license or passport, you'll need to produce one when asked for it. Always customize your cover letter to the company you are applying to; never use a boilerplate form letter. The effort, or lack thereof shows, and does make a difference.

If you have job gaps, use a different type of resume than a chronological resume. Consider hiring a professional resume writer to help create different versions. You can also find free resume help online by searching for 'free resume help', at www.pongoresume.com, or my website www.dedominic.com.

Q:

What
are
Keywords?

A:

Keywords are terms frequently used in your profession to describe special qualities.

Use keywords in your skill based or chronological resume. Examples are software programs, social media, industry specific terms, special qualifications, and certifications.

Recruiters rely on technology to sort through thousands of leads, and are looking for specific skills, people, and employers. Understanding and highlighting your special skills increases your earning power.

Remember to list those valuable skills on any applications you may fill out. If you learned some technical or specialized skills while volunteering, listing them is a good way to leverage this training. Proof read your resume and have a trusted friend or professional review it before sending it out.

Q:

Is it truly *dog eat dog* everyone for themself in this job market?

A:

It does not pay to be a *lone ranger* in the job hunt game.

Today's workplace leverages teams of people organized around projects, much like the movie making process. People have specialties and must be able to work independently, as well as collaborate in teams.

Planting the seeds of opportunity starts with being a friend to others, and cultivating strong alliances. Build and use your own success team to help in your job hunt. Four eyes can see more than two, twenty eyes and ears keeping their radar tuned for job leads will end up finding lots of opportunities.

Look for job hunting friends and groups, but be careful not to join or become a 'sorry club'. Teams pay dividends.

Q:

Should I focus on *job interviews* or *consulting opportunities?*

A:

Both! Sometimes consulting is used as a trial to see if a long-term fit, and regular employment will work.

It is common for some companies to use a pay-rolling service for new staffers, during a trial period. In the new world of work your income opportunities could come in many forms: employee, consultant or freelancer.

If you do become a consultant, be sure to talk to your tax advisor. They can tell you how much to put aside for social security, personal taxes, and what expenses (car, work supplies, uniforms) might be tax deductible.

Q:

How many interviews will it take?

A:

There is no magic number, go on lots of interviews.

The more you audition for your future leading role, the faster you will Land It!

Constantly find places to interview. As you get better, you will increase your options and confidence. You will also get some good feedback.

Employers try to avoid desperate people. Try to show that you are interested and that you are considering other opportunities too. Send a sincere thank you note.

Keep a job log of places you have applied to and follow up with the best opportunities. Stay upbeat. You always want to be optimistic and eager, but you never want to appear desperate. Practice confidence building techniques and your elevator pitch.

Q:

I'd like a change from my old life should I switch careers?

A:

Learn as much as you can about industries and companies that interest you and the skills needed.

You've got homework to do now. Talk to as many people as you can in your preferred job or field. Don't be afraid to ask to do an informational interview. An informational interview is one which gathers general information, makes friends, and increases your network; do this in addition to applying for specific job openings. Learn as much as you can about what is valued in this particular industry. How does this company perceive value? Ask and answer these questions and you are halfway there.

Find informational videos online at Lynda.com. There are many free podcasts, videos, webinars, and blogs produced by successful professionals, talking about their work and their passions. Take advantage of this rich source for preparation, and to determine if switching careers is right for you.

Q:

I'm desperate for a job. Should I take the *first paying offer* I receive?

A:

Yes,
if it fits
with your goals!

Some say it is easier to land your next job when you are currently employed. You should accept the offer when it fits well with your short term or long term goals.

Ask lots of questions. If you have done your homework, researched about the company and the job, you are more likely to recognize good opportunities when you see them.

We do caution about simply accepting the first job offered, if the fit isn't right. This will work against you in the long run. Changing jobs too often, without a great reason, or a fabulous new opportunity, will damage your professional reputation.

"Follow the interests of your mind and heart. Then work, work, work."

Henrietta Holsman Fore
President Holsman International
Former Director of the United States Mint,
U.S. Treasury Department

Q:

My industry has changed again, how can I keep up?

A:

Keep getting valuable experience for your chosen profession to stay competitive.

Read more and stay abreast of industry news and trends. Doing related volunteer work can help you stay fresh and build your network. You can find needed information in a variety of places. Sources of data on your preferred job can be found on US Department of Labor, trade associations, at your local Chamber of Commerce, on experts' blogs, and news online.

Employers often post skill requirements on their website. If you are in school, your career center office or library will have reference materials for you.

The Department of Labor website has information such as average wages, number of hires in each occupation by region, state, and across the country. Visit www.dol.gov.

Being busy isn't enough. Focus and a commitment to continually renewing your skills is essential for staying employed.

"Employers need qualified people with the ability to change with the business environment. Maintaining a strong positive attitude is a key to a successful career. Listening to the needs of the business and developing skills to meet future requirements of the company will make you invaluable."

Robert T. Bouttier
Automobile Club of Southern California

Q:

What is the best resume type for me, since I have so much experience to show?

A:

That depends on your experience.

If you have over 20 years of experience, you may want to use a skills and accomplishments based resume. If you have fewer than 20 years of experience, then use a chronological resume, listing the most recent or most relevant employment first. You may wish to make a video resume for yourself. Some people, particularly those in creative fields, are making themselves stand out this way. You can see examples www.visualcv.com.

Remember social media sites are living, virtual resumes that need regular maintenance. Don't neglect them and get left in last century's economy. Many employers and recruiters rely heavily on these tools. Executive recruiters frequently search LinkedIn groups and keywords, so make sure your profiles are up to date. We live in a keyword world, so it pays to be a bit of a name dropper on your profile and resume.

Q:

What do I do about *work gaps* in my resume?

A:

Use a skills-based resume that features your more in demand skills.

Include a short narrative of your accomplishments. It is common for students, stay-at-home mothers, or care givers to have employment gaps. Don't be afraid to put all your best traits, skills, and most relevant experience up front. You can explain gaps later, if you are asked.

Be honest and focus on what you feel you can do for the employer. This is another good reason to cultivate strong personal referral networks, which may look at your resume but not rely on it. Who you are comes across in these personal referrals, rather than what you look like on paper. Both matter.

Q:

What *mind set* change can I expect in the workforce that *didn't* exist 20 years ago?

A:

It's a So-Lo-Mo world. Social, Local and Mobile rule!

Being qualified may not be enough to land job offers in this competitive environment. Prime of lifers may yearn for the good ole days of face time; today it is more like Facebook time! Texting, voice over IP, video conferencing, and social networking are all essential parts of today's professional environment.

Things often happen at the speed of light, due to advanced technology and access to information. Flexibility, resiliency, and resourcefulness are more important than ever, and employers can't afford any warm bodies.

We now have one of the most diverse work forces with more women and men of all ages holding executive and professional leadership positions in all sectors.

Many of today's businesses have adopted a zero tolerance policy towards discrimination of any kind. There is no place for sexist or discriminatory language or off color jokes. Remember nothing you send out on email or Twitter or other social media is really private.

Q:

Are
thank you letters
old fashioned?

A:

No!

Please remember to send thank you letters. Email is okay, handwritten letters are even better.

A sincere expression of your gratitude is good manners and good business. Even though we now live in a digital age with robots and seemingly impersonal computers, relationships and manners still make a big difference.

Q:

**Should I try
to be *part-time*
or get hired
as a *consultant*
if full time job offers
aren't coming in now?**

A:

Part time and temporary jobs are a great way to get your foot in the door.

You may be able to enter new fields by being more flexible about part time and temporary jobs. You may wish to register with both local and virtual agencies. This is a great way to get a job quickly, enlarge your network, and build new skills. It also lets employers see you, and try before they buy. Talk with your staffing firm representative to see if they serve clients and occupations that are a good fit for you.

Try to have this conversation face to face, it will help the interviewer remember you!

Q:

How do I interview with someone younger and less experienced?

A:

Always be polite, upbeat, and ask and answer questions.

Interviewers come in all ages, shapes and sizes. You will interview with a younger and possibly green manager the same way you handle yourself in any professional situation.

Be open and courteous. Be careful not to come across as condescending to any interviewer. Your next job offer might come from someone half your age. This is where your confidence and life experience can add real value. Look for ways in which you can contribute to your next job no matter how young your new boss is.

Treat all interviewers and staff as if they were your most important customer, they may just become that!

Q:

How do I analyze my skills objectively?

A:

Look to people in your network to provide trusted objective feedback.

This is a time to do some personal reflection, and to get lots of good input. Choose your coaches and mentors carefully, and pay attention to feedback from young people in your life. Choose those who have a positive outlook on life for the best source of motivation and inspiration.

Ask yourself what the marketplace is paying for your skills and remember that value is often in the eye of the customer. The market votes for you with job offers. Count your votes and enhance your skills and openness to *Land It*! Read professional journals and e-zines, ask your network, and your job coach for feedback. Use online resources to analyze your skills at: www.wikihow.com/Analyze-Your-Skills-and-Job-Options.

Q:

How much *money* should I *expect to make?*

A:

Wages vary depending on geography, supply, and skill sets required.

Generally, medical and technological fields pay more. Do your research to learn about your chosen field and location. Talk to people who are already working in your desired field. Find competitive pay at your local Employment Development Department, job club, or at www.salary.com. You can also do some market research, by reading the help wanted job postings online and in newspapers.

The Ladders.com is a web service that offers jobs over $100,000 per year. If you want to increase your income, learn to monitor the offerings, and requirements for these higher paying jobs.

Q:

How do I know if I can trust online resume submission companies?

A:

Ask your network of friends and colleagues about where they found success.

Getting referrals for resume writers and resume submission companies, or staffing firms is the best way to find a good source for you. Beware of total strangers with income schemes that sound too good to be true, most likely they are.

If in doubt, call the firm or Google them to get more information and insight into their general reputation. Use caution, and do not send off too much personal information (credit info, etc.), until you know who you are dealing with.

Q:

How can I avoid falling victim to fake/fraudulent job postings?

A:

If it seems too good to be true it probably is.

As online resources become more and more popular with job seekers, so too does the likelihood of encountering fake or fraudulent job postings. It is important to be aware of how to avoid falling victim to these scams; because the consequences can be quite severe. Pursuing fake job postings or scams can result in signing up for an unwanted product or service, or worse identity theft.

If you inquire or apply for a job posting on an Internet job resource and the poster requests things like: a credit check, personal information (Social Security Number, bank account details), or other important information, use *extreme caution*.

Do your due diligence. Rather than blindly providing them with what they ask, do some research on the company.

Q:

Should I use an *executive recruiter*, *headhunter*, or *staffing agency* in my job hunt?

A:

Yes!

Your job is to reach out to every potential hiring source or circle of influence. Find the firms that specialize in your location, profession, or industry. Register and interview at several to get more interviewing experience. You will want to show off your exceptional hire-ability, and practice your elevator speech.

These intermediaries can be useful for you, and should be considered an important part of your circle of resources.

Executive recruiters are usually retained, or paid by the employer, not the job hunter, remember that they do not necessarily work for you. A recruiter's livelihood depends on assembling, and placing many of qualified people. Talk to lots of them and gain important market intelligence, as well as referrals.

Q:

What are the odds that I'll get a corporate gig with benefits?

A:

99.7% of all employer firms, employing just over half of all private sector employees, are small businesses.

According to the U.S. Small Business Administration, 64% of net new jobs created in the past 15 years were created by small businesses, with sales under $25 million per year.

While small business, education, and government account for more jobs than corporate America; you can get a good job with a major corporation and full benefits, if you focus your interviews there. Benefits vary considerably in small enterprises. Research as much as you can about an employer before you apply.

Many firms list a menu of employee benefits on their websites, and some have very generous packages, which could include: education tuition assistance, paid time off, meals, transportation help, medical, dental insurance, and retirement assistance.

Q:

Should I look at *multiple sources* of Income?

A:

A number of *professionals* told us that they also have *part time jobs, for extra cash or benefits.*

As long as it does not conflict with your primary job, then we believe that successful professionals should strive for multiple sources of income.

Once you're working again, you will want to begin, or upgrade your monthly retirement savings plan.

I've also seen some people exchange work for equity in startups and small ventures. This can pay off occasionally.

Q:

Are there government programs that *help* people in the *prime of their life* looking for a job?

A:

Yes!

In most big cities and communities the Work Force Investment Board has special services for displaced, special needs, and older workers. We suspect you have been investing into this system for many years, as you paid your income taxes.

You may as well tap into these important investments that your tax dollars are making, visit www.onestop.gov. There are many government and community resources ready to help those who truly want to get back to work.

Q:

Is there another non-traditional way for me to get a job?

A:

Networking and volunteer referrals are the biggest source of job offers.

Hiring statistics show that more jobs are filled by referrals from insiders. Many jobs never get posted or advertised. Your friends, family, customers, and vendors are a good source of job-hunting intelligence. Good leads and referrals will also come from the big job boards like Monster.com, your local newspaper, the EDD, your local Chamber of Commerce, as well as your church, job clubs, or support groups. Volunteers often learn about paying job leads long before they are posted.

Another great source of referrals is your alumni association, school career centers and employment agencies, leave no stone unturned. Provide yourself with the best options, and the most leads. Look beyond the obvious sources, and you will find your leads multiplying.

Q:

I've had a lot of *rejections,* and trouble even getting called for interviews. How do I *rebuild my* confidence?

A:

Keep on learning, practice your elevator pitch, and look for ways to increase your contacts.

Surround yourself with positive people, who are also committed to learning new skills. Make a list of some of your career or life accomplishments.

Start a list of things you are grateful for. It doesn't have to be long, even 3 or 4 items is a good start. Reviewing this list, and expanding as you think of other things that give you pleasure and success, will help you list skills you can contribute to your next workplace.

Get out and get some exercise and fresh air. When you take a break to smell the roses, you give yourself a real boost.

Some quotes are timeless and were reprinted from my first book, The New World of Work.

Special thanks to:

Paul Orfalea, Fed-Ex Kinkos

Henrietta Holsman Fore, US Mint

Robert T. Bouttier, Automobile Club

Mayor Jim Delshad, City of Beverly Hills

APPENDIX

The Bare Basics
of Computer Literacy

Typing: Learning a computer keyboard, and typing at 40 words per minute (wpm) or more will help you.

Microsoft Word: is a word processing program which will enable you to do memos, letters, and documents.

Outlook: One of the most common email programs, which allows you to manage mail, contacts (Rolodex), and calendar tasks.

Cut/Copy/Paste: This shortcut helps you move or change documents. It is a basic that may seem like everyone can do, but novices may not even know about this time saver practice.

File sharing: using Google Documents, Go to My PC, GoToMeeting, Dropbox, or other methods to share work with others, are tools now in daily use.

Microsoft Excel: will enable you to make spreadsheets with tables, and is also a basic accounting program.

Internet Browsing: You will need to be able to do research on the Internet. Almost anything you want to know about any employer is now online.

Even if you don't own a computer, you can access one daily for no cost at your public library, for a small fee at an internet café, or at office printing shops like Fed-Ex Kinkos.

Job Hunting 101 Checklist

Check all that apply:

☐ Objective Clarified

☐ Resume & Cover Letter

☐ Resume & Cover Letter Proofread Twice

☐ References Prepared

☐ Computer Skills Updated

☐ Transportation & Communication Arranged

☐ Prepared and Able to Work

☐ Strengths and Weaknesses Defined

☐ Proper Attire for the Job

☐ Attitude Adjusted and Focused

☐ Mentors or Job Counselors Consulted

☐ Elevator Pitch Ready

Tally Your Score: _____

John Smith

jsmith@email.com
123 Easy Street
Anytown, USA, 93110
805-555-5555

Career Objective

To obtain a marketing position with an advertising agency that will utilize my sales background and my interpersonal communication skills.

Sales Skills

- Contributed to the increase of the average dollar sale at the retail level through product knowledge, demonstration, and point-of-sale interactions.
- Participated in group oriented project to prepare marketing and promotional materials for advertising for the purpose of recruiting new members into the college's Student Alumni Association.

Communication Skills

- Created and edited press releases for a Pittsburgh-based hospital; composed feature, sports, and editorial pieces for the University student newspaper.
- Conducted weekly meetings and presentations with fraternity representatives and Greek Life Coordinator in preparation for Rush, which involved several hundred students.

Organizational and Managerial Skills

- Handled purchases and returns, and prepared in-store marketing for a national retail corporation. Trained new employees, performed business transactions.
- Worked directly with Greek Life Coordinator for one year to coordinate and facilitate fraternity rush.
- Effectively acclimated a community of 20 undergraduate freshmen to college life through regular interpersonal and group contact, educational and social programming, and enforcement of college policy.

Work History

University Hospital	Anytown, USA	2005-2011
Communications Department		
Linen's N Things	Anytown, USA	1997-1999
Sales Associate		
University	Anytown, USA	1999-2005
Resident Assistant		
Blue Ginger Restaurant	Anytown, USA	1985-1999
Manager		

Education

University   Anytown, USA
Bachelor of Arts Degree
Major: Sales   Minor: Marketing   Cumulative GPA 3.0/4.0

John Smith

jsmith@email.com
123 Easy Street
Anytown, USA, 93110
805-555-5555

Qualifications for Accounting Clerk

Diagnostic and problem-solving MBA with accounting and clerical support experience under $42 billion company. Commended for processing ability, auditing accounts payable, reconciling debs and credits, and strength in devising creative presentations using Microsoft tools. Up-to-date on latest challenges facing accounting firms and risk management. Adept at devising cost-saving methods.

Ares of expertise include: Supply Purchasing, Interpersonal Communications, Generally Accepted Accounting Principles, Payroll, Budgeting, Account Research/Tracking, Financial Standards Accounting Board Regulations, Problem Resolution, Document Filing/Updating, General Ledger Worksheets, Retro Payments, and Document Development.

Analytical Background

Accounting Clerk: ABC Enterprises, Anytown, USA   2005 – 2011

Apply detail-oriented mindset to providing accounting and clerical support for $42 billion international servicer of aeronautics, electronic systems, information systems, global services, and space systems. Audit and process Veterans of Armed Forces accounts for VA retro pay benefits. Utilize Excel spreadsheets to calculate retro payments. Handle various case types, including Method A, CRSC (Combat Related Special Compensation), CRDP (Concurrent Retired Disability Pay), blended (CRSC/CRDP), Reservist. Accessed Federal databases to gather information. Resolve special case situations, including debit and credit circumstances. Develop debits and credits for designated members. Enter payroll-related information to MS Access database.

Accomplishments

- Selected to join Specialty Team to process in-depth cases that required non-typical research. Served on team of 20 top Processors selected out of 200 employees in department.
- Promoted to permanent Accounting Clerk role as a result of outstanding processing skills.
- Processed on average six cases daily (with department goal of 3 daily). Possessed average score of more than 90% pass rate against company maximum rate of 85%.
- Ensured untapped government funds were distributed accurately and expediently through VA retro pay program to Veterans of Armed Forces.

Accounting Clerk: University, Anytown, USA   1990 – 2005

Supported the accounting operations of the bookkeeper in the Plant Pathology Department. Created and verified the accuracy of reports used for budge analysis. Coordinated files; ensured accessibility and verified accuracy of information. Administered departmental invoices and compared account, project, and object data with the availability of funds in accordance with College of Agriculture and Life Sciences (CALS) and NCSU guidelines.

Accomplishments

- Maintained invoice data using PeopleSoft and performed budget checks to route for approval. Managed files to ensure approval of vouchers, acquired status of approval requests, and forwarded vouchers to accounts payable daily.
- Evaluated vendor invoices and settled all unpaid invoices.
- Recognized as the primary point of contact on Web-based travel reimbursement process. Assessed reimbursements for accuracy and verified appropriate funding availability.

Credentials

Master of Business Administration, Accountancy, University – Anytown, USA
Bachelor of Arts, Accounting, University – Anytown USA

John Smith

jsmith@email.com
123 Easy Street
Anytown, USA, 93110
805-555-5555

Career Objective

To obtain a career as a manager in a health and fitness oriented environment.

Related Experience

Fitness Instructor   1996-2011

University Fitness Center, Anytown, USA
- Assisted instructor with exercise fitness programs (20 hours weekly).
- Led and instructed 27 aerobics participants and integrated exercise data.

Practicum Experience

University Wellness Center, Anytown, USA   2006-2011
- Coordinated and led group exercises; administered warm up and cool down exercises.
- Assisted with fitness testing and recommended exercise plan.
- Presented educational seminars on stress management.

Strength and Conditioning Trainer

Youth Training Center, Anytown, USA   1990-1996
- Developed conditioning programs for youth ages 12-17.
- Assisted conditioning coach with supervision of speed and endurance programs and recorded as well as maintained strength and conditioning data.

Sales Representative

Jim's Sporting Goods, Anytown, USA   1979-1990
- Train new employees in day-to-day operations.
- Responsible for store opening and closing procedures.
- Contribute to increased customer sales through extensive product knowledge.
- Provide superior customer service to patrons.

Certifications and Professional Designations

CPR and First Aid certification, American Red Cross, Anytown, USA   1990

Education

University/College, Anytown, USA
Bachelor of Science

Major: Physical Education	Major GPA: 4.0/4.0	Cumulative GPA: 3.4/4.0
Academic Honors		
Dean's List 2 Semesters		Honors Program Fall 19XX – spring 19XX

Related Academic Projects
Weight Reduction and Stress Management Project: worked with a group of volunteer candidates on a weight reduction program that emphasizes stress management techniques.

Notes & Follow Up Action Steps

Notes & Follow Up Action Steps

_____

_____

_____

_____

_____

_____

_____

_____

_____

_____

_____

_____

_____

_____

_____

_____

_____

_____

_____

_____

_____

_____

Notes & Follow Up Action Steps

Notes & Follow Up Action Steps

Notes & Follow Up Action Steps

_____

_____

_____

_____

_____

_____

_____

_____

_____

_____

_____

_____

_____

_____

_____

_____

_____

_____

_____

_____

_____

_____

_____

Notes & Follow Up Action Steps

_____

_____

_____

_____

_____

_____

_____

_____

_____

_____

_____

_____

_____

_____

_____

_____

_____

_____

_____

_____

_____

_____

Notes & Follow Up Action Steps

Notes & Follow Up Action Steps

Notes & Follow Up Action Steps

Notes & Follow Up Action Steps

_____

_____

_____

_____

_____

_____

_____

_____

_____

_____

_____

_____

_____

_____

_____

_____

_____

_____

_____

_____

_____

_____

_____

_____

Interview Notes

Date	Company Name:		Position	Thank You
	Interviewer:			
Phone:			Follow Up:	
E-mail:			Next Steps:	
Additional Notes:				

Date	Company Name:		Position	Thank You
	Interviewer:			
Phone:			Follow Up:	
E-mail:			Next Steps:	
Additional Notes:				

Date	Company Name:		Position	Thank You
	Interviewer:			
Phone:			Follow Up:	
E-mail:			Next Steps:	
Additional Notes:				

Interview Notes

Date	Company Name:	Position	Thank You
	Interviewer:		
Phone:		Follow Up:	
E-mail:		Next Steps:	
Additional Notes:			

Date	Company Name:	Position	Thank You
	Interviewer:		
Phone:		Follow Up:	
E-mail:		Next Steps:	
Additional Notes:			

Date	Company Name:	Position	Thank You
	Interviewer:		
Phone:		Follow Up:	
E-mail:		Next Steps:	
Additional Notes:			

Interview Notes

Date	Company Name:		Position	Thank You
	Interviewer:			
Phone:			Follow Up:	
E-mail:			Next Steps:	
Additional Notes:				

Date	Company Name:		Position	Thank You
	Interviewer:			
Phone:			Follow Up:	
E-mail:			Next Steps:	
Additional Notes:				

Date	Company Name:		Position	Thank You
	Interviewer:			
Phone:			Follow Up:	
E-mail:			Next Steps:	
Additional Notes:				

Interview Notes

Date	Company Name:		Position	Thank You
	Interviewer:			
Phone:			Follow Up:	
E-mail:			Next Steps:	
Additional Notes:				

Date	Company Name:		Position	Thank You
	Interviewer:			
Phone:			Follow Up:	
E-mail:			Next Steps:	
Additional Notes:				

Date	Company Name:		Position	Thank You
	Interviewer:			
Phone:			Follow Up:	
E-mail:			Next Steps:	
Additional Notes:				

Patty DeDominic

While Patty DeDominic ran her placement business, she and her team successfully placed over 250,000 people in a variety of industries across the country. She sold that business in 2006 to a firm that grew to over a billion dollars in annual sales.

DeDominic perfected winning formulas for making higher quality job placements. The companies she worked with were very successful. Patty's companies, PDQ Careers and CT Engineering, developed a strong reputation for extraordinary commitment to people, integrity and professionalism.

Leading employers such as Microsoft, Wells Fargo Bank, AT&T, USC, Harvard, Western, Stanford, and many private and public universities, hospitals, foundations as well as the US Department of Labor and the Small Business Administration (SBA) came to trust the DeDominic Team's advice and use her recruitment services.

www.DeDominic.com

www.ingramcontent.com/pod-product-compliance
Lightning Source LLC
Chambersburg PA
CBHW051538170526
45165CB00002B/785